The Anatomy of Success & Failure

7 Essential Elements that will
Guarantee Radical Success in Life!

John Di Lemme

The Anatomy of Success and Failure
Copyright © 2013 John Di Lemme

Di Lemme Development Group, Inc.
931 Village Boulevard
Suite 905-366
West Palm Beach, Florida 33409-1939
(888) 567-0717
www.LifestyleFreedomClub.com

This book is designed to provide competent and reliable information regarding the subject matters covered. However, it is sold with the understanding that the author is not engaged in rendering legal, financial, or other professional advice. Laws and practices often vary from state to state and if legal or other expert assistance is required, the services of a professional should be sought. The author specifically disclaims any liability that is incurred from the use and/or application of the contents of this book.

ISBN: 978-1-300-70101-9

About the Author

In September 2001, John Di Lemme founded Di Lemme Development Group, Inc., a company known worldwide for its role in expanding the personal development industry. As President and CEO, John strives for excellence in every area of his business and believes that you must surround yourself with a like-minded team in order to stay on top of your game.

In addition to building a successful company, John has changed lives around the globe as an international motivational speaker that has spoken in over five hundred venues. Over the past eleven years, he has shared the stage with the best of the best including Dr. John Maxwell, Rich Devos, Dennis Waitley, Jim Rohn, and Les Brown only to name a few. John has also been interviewed countless times and featured on many programs including Zig Ziglar's webcast. This is truly an amazing feat for someone that was clinically diagnosed as a stutterer at a very young age and told that he would never speak fluently.

John truly believes that everyone needs personal development to reach their full potential in life, and his determination to reach all forms of media with his motivational messages has catapulted his career. John has produced over four hundred fifty products and is an accomplished author of eleven books including his latest best-selling book, "7 Principles to Live a Champion Life." As a Strategic Business Coach, John's students include doctors, lawyers, entrepreneurs, consultants, CEOs of million dollar companies and various other occupations that are thriving in a so-called poor economy. John's success with his students has made him one of the most highly sought after business coaches in the world.

John's passion is to teach others how to live a champion life despite the label that society has placed on them. Through his books, audio/video materials, sold-out live seminars, numerous television interviews, intensive training boot camps, weekly tele-classes, Strategic Business Coaching, Closing & Marketing University, Millionaire Affirmation Academy, and Lifestyle Freedom Club memberships, John has made success a reality for thousands worldwide.

Introduction

When you hear the word "anatomy", what do you think about? Do you think of the body and what you actually see? How it's made up, the structures, what's there? Sometimes even with visible anatomy, if someone has an illness or sickness, they may have to go in for an X-ray or an MRI and dig a little deeper to determine what is wrong. We're going to dig down deep into the anatomy of success and failure because success and failure are exactly the same. They're simply results. In the Greek, the word "anatomy" means 'cutting up – to cut up'. So, we are going to cut up what is deep inside of success and failure.

Most of you reading this book are entrepreneurs and business owners. In my book, *177 Motivational Success Quotes to Live the Championship Life,* the very first quote has nothing to do with money. It's lifestyle freedom. It's the ability to do what you want to do, when you want to do it with whoever you want to do it with as long as you like to do it. That's called freedom and freedom is either success or you're not free because you start to live in failure. As an entrepreneur and business owner it's very important to recognize that point.

When I asked you the question about what you think of when I say the word 'anatomy', you probably thought of the body. You think of the finished product. You think of an adult. In the doctor's office, they usually have the little skeleton there which is the anatomy of the body. Keep a mental picture of that skeleton that is sitting in the doctor's office. The anatomy of success and failure is really parallel with the physical world, the mental world, the emotional world because without a vertebra, your body would have a problem. You would have a major issue without blood. There are 111 bones in one foot alone. But if one is broken a little bit, you're limping.

A lot of times in life, failures are limping and eventually the limp becomes a lifestyle and then you accept the failure. As we dig down deep into success, you really must understand and accept that you have to take responsibility, either for your success or for your failure.

For the last 12 years, I've seen people come out to events and be fired up and excited. And then I've seen them quit. They get to one of the steps required for success and all of a sudden they think, "No, I can't do that." They reject it and then they make an excuse and they quit. No one has ever come back to me in five years and said, "John, I did the complete opposite of what you strategically coached me on and I'm successful."

Here's a homework assignment for you before you go any further in this book. I want you to write, "Coach Di Lemme, I'm committed to the five-year process! Today's date is *(fill in the date),* and I will stand strong for the next five years. I am fully committed to my success!" Now here's what I want you to do. I want you to e-mail it to John@LifestyleFreedomClub.com and print one out for yourself.

Put your commitment in front of you so that you see it every day, because there will be a day that you are pushed to choose between success and failure. It's a continuous reminder of what you are fighting for in life. It will remind you to choose success no matter what you face. If you choose failure, then rip up your commitment with a full understanding that you have given up on success and your ability to achieve it.

It's very important to have clarity and have a sense of accomplishment in front of you. This is the foundation. It's like having your birth certificate in front of you. When you keep this in front of you, it will eventually get inside you and you will realize that at one time, you were born a Champion with the absolute right to be a success.

We were all children at one time. Notice the process from birth to five years old. It's a growth process for the human body. Similarly, there's a success process. That's very important to know, because of the five year commitment that you've printed out and hung in front of you. When you choose to follow all of the strategies that I'm going to review in depth in this book, success is going to happen. It's inevitable for you not to grow in the success process just like it's nearly impossible for a healthy human body not to grow if it's being feed and nourished in its growth process.

Another definition of anatomy is *a detailed analysis*. Now, let's take it a little further. To analyze something means that you are breaking it down into essential elements. For example, if one essential element is missing from a recipe, it's not going to taste good, right? It would be like leaving the cheese out of the macaroni and cheese. It changes the entire recipe, because it's missing an essential element.

Unfortunately, most people's lives are missing the essential elements that make up success. They aren't willing to take the extra steps needed so that they achieve the level of success that they've always dreamed of. They keep trying to take shortcuts in the success process.

Have you ever heard someone say, "Well, you don't know me. I am stuck in my ways." Let me tell you about 'My Way'. It's a Frank Sinatra song but it's also an excuse. People say, "I'm stuck in my own way," which means they are in their own way and can't move forward. It's an excuse!

I'm going to give you seven essential elements for success and if you are willing to step aside from doing things your way, then you will progress towards your Why in the success process and fully understand the anatomy of success and failure. But it all comes down to your commitment. Now, let's get started.

Essential Element #1: Make the Decision to Succeed

You make the decision that you want to succeed. That's it! It's simply a decision. I went to a business event at the Rye Town Hilton, on March 15, 1990, and I made a decision that night to succeed. I made a decision to become a highly successful entrepreneur. On my way home, I was fired up about my future! I called my best friend to share my excitement. The first thing he said to me was "Stay away from those people. That's not real." He was my closest friend! He said, "That's not going to work. That's just not real." I made a decision to succeed that night, but I could have allowed him to change my mind.

He could have made a decision for me to fail, but I stood up for my dream and made a decision to succeed. Similarly, everyone that has failed in life, made a decision in some way or another to fail. They made a decision to give up, to quit, to just say, "It's not for me. You don't know where I come from." or "That's too good to be true."

Now, let me clarify something. I'm not talking about taking a risk and failing at something. We've all done that and it's an important part of our success journey. I'm referring to the type of failure that is decision based and stops you from achieving the level of success that you deserve. That's why the first Essential Element is so important. You have to make a rock-solid decision to succeed or you will instantly make a decision to fail. It is incredibly powerful!

Essential Element #2: Be Willing

There are two main areas in success that people have a challenge with – willingness to learn and willingness to listen. One of my daily habits is I make sure that I'm willing to listen and I'm willing to learn. Yes, every single day!

Some of my greatest learning experiences have come from listening to and watching people that have made the decision to fail. No, I don't recommend that you commit to do this daily, but it's an interesting process for me as a Strategic Millionaire Business Coach. Let me explain.

Failure is success going backwards. People that choose failure over success take the same yet opposite actions of a champion that has made a decision to succeed. They build their own mastermind team *(negative associations instead of positive);* they immerse themselves in books, CDs, DVDs, TV and other forms of media *(all negative news and information);* and they have daily habits that they engage in every single day *(negative habits that drive them further from their dream).* Failure is the flip side of everything that you are willing to do as a champion that made the decision to succeed.

Now, I know you're saying, "John, what does that have to do with me and my willingness? I'm not like those people." Let me put it to you straight. Yes, you are if you don't make the decision to be willing to listen and learn every single day, even if it's something you don't want to hear. Ahh...I got your attention on that one!

I guarantee that you will have record breaking results when you start listening to and learning from the things that you don't want to hear. Deep down inside you know that you need to hear them and need to change. You have to drop the ego and be willing to grow outside of your comfort zone. Now, that's what I call being willing to listen and learn.

Everyone has that one special event in life that gives them a huge opportunity to listen and learn to the point that it changes their life completely. For me, it was overcoming my stuttering disability. I went to grammar school in Yonkers, New York. I still remember walking down Tuckahoe Road on my way to school getting lost in my thoughts and questioning God as to why I couldn't talk without stuttering. What I didn't know was that God had a plan for my life and used stuttering to drive me towards that plan.

As a stutterer, I was forced to listen and learn more than the average child. I honed those skills to excel in speaking and communication, which has led me to be one of the most sought after motivational speakers in the world. But it wasn't my choice. I was forced to listen and learn by my adversity.

Everyone has been through something in life that made them ask the question, "Why me?" In order to fully understand why you are going through something in your life, you must be willing to listen and learn just like I did with my stuttering or you may miss the opportunity that lies deep within your adversity. I don't believe that anything happens by coincidence, not even the problems that we face, so make sure that you are always willing to close your mouth, open your ears and learn despite your feelings about the actual situation.

Essential Element #3: Appreciate Your Struggle

Appreciating your struggle isn't always easy, especially when you are usually fighting to get out of the situation that is causing the struggle. One of my favorite definitions of struggle is *to advance with violent effort.*

Imagine a butterfly fighting to shed its cocoon. Without the cocoon, the caterpillar would never go through the season to turn into a beautiful butterfly. As the butterfly fights its way out of the cocoon, its wings grow stronger and stronger so that it can fly free from captivity. However, when most people see a butterfly, they appreciate its beauty and are not even remotely aware of the struggle that it had to go through to become such an amazing creature.

Are You a Member of the #1 Success & Motivation Club?
Check It Out Now – www.LifestyleFreedomClub.com
7 Highly Controversial Motivational Teachings FREE

Similarly, success is always hidden by challenges and problems. In solving them, you acquire the skills that you need to excel in every area of your life and achieve your ultimate Why. Sadly, many of us are not willing to struggle to shed the cocoon that is holding us captive. We get comfortable in the cocoon, which leads to the failure to move forward and reach the next level of success.

Many people are struggling right now in business because they are simply not focused. Instead of facing the struggle and appreciating the strength that they gain from the fight, they whine, moan and complain about it. There's nothing worse than a whiner that is literally holding opportunity in the palm of their hands, but they won't pay the price to get it.

Olympic Gold Medalist Nikki Stone is a great personal friend of mine. She broke her back two years prior to winning a gold medal and ten doctors told her she would never walk. They told her one thing that would have made most people quit, but she told herself something different. She made a decision to struggle. Nikki fought through her adversity and won a gold medal.

Fighting is part of the struggle no matter if you like it or not. It's not pretty and it's not easy, but it's part of what you have to do to succeed. What if that butterfly said, "You know what, I'm just going to hang out here in the cocoon a little bit longer. I just want to go back to being a caterpillar, because all this fighting is too much." That would be impossible, because the caterpillar is gone forever. There's no turning back! It has to

Are You a Member of the #1 Success & Motivation Club?
Check It Out Now – www.LifestyleFreedomClub.com
7 Highly Controversial Motivational Teachings FREE

keep going no matter how hard and long the fight might be.

I once heard a man describe trying to help a butterfly get free of its cocoon. He took a knife and cut the cocoon away. The butterfly came out but then died right before his eyes. That butterfly needed to struggle to survive. It simply didn't have the strength to face the world without the struggle.

We all need to struggle. You have to appreciate it and focus on what's on the other side of the fight. You will finally be free from captivity! Remember, you can't speed up the struggle. The fight may be long and hard, but never give up no matter how long it takes to break free from your cocoon.

Essential Element #4: Blind Bamboo Faith

The next Essential Element is BBF, which stands for blind bamboo faith. Now, let me explain, because I know you are likely really confused by those three little words.

Interestingly, it takes five to six years for the bamboo to just break ground, but within one day, it could grow up to eighty feet. After a year or two in the growth process, the bamboo is so strong that hunters actually use it to protect themselves from charging rhinos. Can you imagine a plant being so strong that it can sustain a hit from a rhino running at it full force? Now, that's incredible strength!

The important thing to remember is that the bamboo didn't start out like that. It went through a growth process. At one point, it

Are You a Member of the #1 Success & Motivation Club?
Check It Out Now – www.LifestyleFreedomClub.com
7 Highly Controversial Motivational Teachings FREE

was just a small seed. The bamboo didn't question the growth process. It waited patiently underground for five or six years being nurtured and fed until it finally saw daylight. With the sun feeding its growth, it quickly developed strength and power. Eventually, it became the mightiest plant in the jungle. Why? Because it had blind bamboo faith. It didn't let its meager beginnings or the fact that it was stuck in darkness for six years determine its ultimate outcome.

Your Why is like a tiny bamboo seed that is deep within the soil. You feed it with nutrients like daily affirmations, and it begins to take on a life of its own. However, most people don't allow their Why to even start the growth cycle. It just stays buried deep in the darkness. Why? Because they lack blind bamboo faith.

For example, one of my Elite Coaching Students, Dorcie Farkash, had her Why *(her ultimate purpose in life)* shoved down deep inside of her heart when we met. She was in search of all kinds of things to make her happy, but she wasn't finding the happiness that she desperately desired because it laid dormant in the darkness. Once Dorcie figured out what her Why really was in life, she started feeding it every day with affirmations. She nurtured it by immersing herself in positive motivational books, CDs, DVDs and other materials. Dorcie became focused on her Why and that seed deep down in her heart started its growth process.

Five years later, Dorcie Farkash is no longer a miserable person in fear of losing everything that she's ever worked for in life.

She's found her happiness. She has strong, healthy relationships with her family. Her business has surpassed the million dollar level. She is mentally, physically and emotionally healthy. She is changing lives through her giving. She is strong enough to stand up to any adversity that stands in her way. Dorcie didn't focus on the darkness. She had blind bamboo faith and now she is achieving all of her dreams and more.

You might be saying, "Well, that's great for her, but I can't see my way out of the darkness to even remotely think about being that happy in life." Remember, that's how Dorcie started out. The only way that having blind bamboo faith won't work for you is if you don't give it a chance and your Why stays buried in darkness for the rest of your life. No one deserves to live like that.

One of the main things that stops you from allowing your Why to grow is other people. You start to get excited about your Why, you feed it daily with affirmations, and you start to immerse yourself in positive personal development materials. You share your excitement with friends and family. Then it happens. The committee of "they" starts to tell you that it will never work, and you are wasting your time. They question your every move and discourage you from continuing the growth process, because it just isn't realistic to them.

You have two choices at this point. Let the naysayers determine your level of success, and you simply allow your Why seed to die. Or you stand up for yourself and your Why with blind bamboo faith. No matter what anyone says to you, you keep

Are You a Member of the #1 Success & Motivation Club?
Check It Out Now – www.LifestyleFreedomClub.com
7 Highly Controversial Motivational Teachings FREE

standing strong with blind bamboo faith. You keep feeding and nourishing your Why. You develop strength to the point that the naysayers can no longer discourage you. Before long, you are living your Why and encouraging those same people that ridiculed you to do the same. This leads right into the next Essential Element.

Essential Element #5: Associations

Your associations absolutely guarantee success or failure. If I were to back-track failure in someone's life, I can almost guarantee that the failure was in some way caused or supported by a negative association in that person's life. Similarly, if I look back on the success journey of my coaching students, I will find people in their lives that supported and encouraged them along the way. They simply couldn't have made it if they didn't have a mastermind team that empowered them to achieve their goals and dreams.

This is serious stuff. Think about it. If you were determined to become physically fit and healthy, you wouldn't continue to keep chips, doughnuts and candy in your pantry. You would implement the gift of good-bye in your diet. How? You would make a conscious decision to move out of the old nutritional neighborhood, and separate yourself from fast food restaurants in order to be elevated to healthy power foods. What if you tried to be healthy but made the decision to keep eating junk food? It simply wouldn't work. You can't have a healthy body by continuing to put toxins in it.

Now, I know you are likely saying, "John, that's common sense. Everyone knows that." If that's true, then why do people that strive for success make the conscious decision to keep the same negative friends? They are ruining your chance at success just like junk food ruins your ability to be healthy.

I'm often asked, "What's the number one reason for success and failure?" Hands down...the answer is associations. It's not a person's inability to achieve success or lack of opportunity in the world. The number one cause of success or failure in a person's life is their mastermind team. Your mastermind team is who you surround yourself with on a daily basis. If you don't know who those people are in your life, just take a look at your cell phone. The top five people that you talk to on a daily basis will determine your level of success or failure. I know that's scary for some people, but whoever you surround yourself with is who you will ultimately become in life.

The reason that I sound like I'm from New York is because I was born and raised there. My mom and dad are New Yorkers. My entire crazy Italian family is from New York. On the flip side, my wife is from

Are You a Member of the #1 Success & Motivation Club?
Check It Out Now – www.LifestyleFreedomClub.com
7 Highly Controversial Motivational Teachings FREE

Tennessee and had a thick Southern accent when we met. Over the years, she has lost some of her accent because she no longer lives in Tennessee plus she is married to a New Yorker. However, when she goes back to Tennessee to spend time with her mother, her accent instantly comes back.

Similarly, if you hang out with positive champions, then you will develop a success accent. Everything that comes out of your mouth will be influenced by your Why and your desire to be successful in life. If you go back to the "old" you, then you will instantly revert back to your old ways and hang out with negative naysayers that condemn your dreams. As you see, your success or failure is determined by your associations.

Making the decision to separate yourself from negative associations will likely be a very lonely time in your life. I call it the isolation zone. You no longer hang out with your old friends, and you haven't built a positive mastermind team yet. This is a very crucial crossroad for your Why. Keep pressing forward no matter how lonely it gets. Stay focused on your dream!

That's the exact reason that I created the Lifestyle Freedom Club. The Club is full of fired up champions just like you that have a desire to be successful. They celebrate each other's successes and support each other through the hard times. If you've had a hard time building your mastermind team and want to surround yourself with other champions, then I suggest that you join the Club. Visit www.LifestyleFreedomClub.com to become a member today!

Are You a Member of the #1 Success & Motivation Club?
Check It Out Now – www.LifestyleFreedomClub.com
7 Highly Controversial Motivational Teachings FREE

Essential Element #6: Structural Integrity

Close your eyes and picture a frozen body of water. It's vast and covered with a wintery blanket of snow. A novice will look at this frozen landscape and conclude that there is no way for a ship to cross it, but that's not true. Large vessels are designed to cut through ice. They're built with structural integrity and strength to grind and cut away at the ice with no problem.

Most people look at obstacles in their lives the same way. They instantly assume that they can't overcome something that big. The word "impossible" is part of their everyday lives. "It's impossible" becomes permission for them to accept failure in everything that challenges them. "It's impossible" is an excuse for not achieving your goals and dreams. You give up before you even try.

Why are so many people stuck in the impossible mindset? It's simple. They lack structural integrity. To face the impossible requires deep-rooted strength that will allow you to push through the impossible just like the large vessels push through the ice. You wouldn't attempt to cross the Arctic in a rubber dingy so why would you attempt to face obstacles in your life with an impossible mindset?

Developing the deep rooted strength that will provide you with the structural integrity that you need to face adversity takes commitment. You must commit to immersing yourself daily in positive self-development, saying your daily affirmations out loud, and associating daily with positive

Are You a Member of the #1 Success & Motivation Club?
Check It Out Now – www.LifestyleFreedomClub.com
7 Highly Controversial Motivational Teachings FREE

champions. Notice the keyword in that sentence – daily. Every single day, you must commit to building that deep rooted strength that will serve as the foundation for your ability to overcome the impossible.

When we talk about the integrity of a ship's hull that has the ability to cut through ice, we are referring to the solid, strong part of the ship that does not bend or compromise when it's busting through ice. The ship's integrity is exactly the same when it enters and exits the ice.

Now, let's compare our integrity. When we face obstacles, our integrity should remain constant. We should not bend or compromise our integrity because of a challenging situation. Unfortunately when it comes to facing the impossible, people suddenly forget everything they stand for and are willing to push aside their values to just get through the situation.

The word "compromise" is defined as *making a dishonorable or shameful concession or decision*. Doesn't it make you cringe to think that your actions have been shameful or dishonorable? But when most people are faced with an impossible situation, they instantly start thinking how they can get around the impossible instead of facing it head on.

That's why I love the Bible story of David and Goliath. When facing a massive giant that seemed impossible to defeat especially since he was only armed with a few stones and a slingshot, David ran directly towards Goliath. He didn't run away or wait for Goliath to attack him. David ran towards the impossible. His structural integrity gave him the confidence to face the impossible and defeat it.

You will face adversity *(the impossible)* in your life. It's inevitable! Dr. Todd Mullins says that if you aren't smack dab in the middle of adversity, then you are likely coming out of it or getting ready to enter it. Simply put...adversity is a part of life. So, you can either face it with sound structural integrity or you will continue to make excuses and let impossibility control your level of success for the rest of your life. Remember, building your structural integrity is a daily process that you must commit to in order to face the enemy of impossible.

Essential Element #7: Brutally Truthful

Last but not least, you have to be brutally truthful with yourself about the thin line between success and failure. No one is immune to failure. That's right. We have all failed at something in our lives. Thomas Edison failed ten thousand times before he finally created the light bulb. Aren't you glad he didn't give up? He understood that just because he failed at something didn't mean he had to stay in the failure zone no matter how many times he failed.

That's the difference between Thomas Edison and so many other people. He didn't take up residence in the failure zone. He was brutally truthful with himself about his failure and he learned from it. Think about failure and how much it hurts. Can you

Are You a Member of the #1 Success & Motivation Club?
Check It Out Now – www.LifestyleFreedomClub.com
7 Highly Controversial Motivational Teachings FREE

imagine the pain that Thomas Edison went through after ten thousand failures? However, he knew his Why and didn't let thousands of failures stand in the way of his success.

Failure scares most people so much that once they fail, they will never try again. They settle for failure. Fear of failure is one of the fastest growing phobias in the world. Why? Because most people lack the ability to fully surrender to the fact that failing is part of the success process not the end result. Instead they wallow in their misery after failing and never try again. They actually stand in the way of their own success.

We've discussed the fact that failure hurts. How do you get past it so you aren't afraid to try and try again until you succeed? I recommend this two step process. First, you become brutally truthful with yourself by admitting your failure. Say it out loud, "I failed! Failure is part of my success journey. I will not remain in the failure zone!" The second step is to stand firm on the structural integrity that you've development through your commitment to daily personal development. This will give you the strength to push through failure so that you can achieve success. The key is to remain brutally truthful about your failure with a full understanding that you absolutely deserve success in every area of your life.

Are You a Member of the #1 Success & Motivation Club?
Check It Out Now – www.LifestyleFreedomClub.com
7 Highly Controversial Motivational Teachings FREE

Conclusion

These seven essential elements will radically explode your level of success if you implement them into your daily action steps. Remember, your birth certificate gives you the absolute right to achieve success. Don't be discouraged by your failures. Instead, allow them to drive you to succeed and stay focused on your Why in life. You are a Champion!

www.ingramcontent.com/pod-product-compliance
Lightning Source LLC
Chambersburg PA
CBHW061520180526
45171CB00001B/258